CONTENTS

HOW TO USE THIS GUIDE

SCOPE AND SEQUENCE

Welcome to the *40 Days Through the Book* study on Ephesians! During the course of the next six weeks, you will embark on an in-depth exploration of the apostle Paul's message to the church in Ephesus. You will learn approximately when he wrote the book, the audience to whom it was written, and the background and context in which it was written. But, more importantly, through the teaching by Derwin Gray, you will explore the key themes that Paul relates in the book—and how they apply to you today.

SESSION OUTLINE

The *40 Days Through the Book* video and study guide are designed to be experienced in a group setting (such as a Bible study, Sunday school class, or small group gathering) and also as an individual study. Each session begins with an introductory reading and one to two ice-breaker type questions. You will then watch a video with Derwin Gray, which can be accessed via the streaming code found on the inside front cover. There is an outline provided in the guide for you to take notes and gather your reflections as you watch the video.

Next, if you are doing this study in a group, you will engage in a time of directed discussion, review the memory verses for the week, and then close each session with a time of personal reflection and prayer. (Note that if your group is larger, you may wish to watch the videos together and then break into smaller groups of four to six people, to ensure that everyone has time to participate in discussions.)

40-DAY JOURNEY

What is truly unique about this study, and all of the other studies in the *40 Days Through the Book* series, are the daily learning resources that will lead you into a deeper engagement with the text. Each week, you will be given a set of daily readings, with accompanying reflection questions, to help you explore the material that you covered during your group time.

The first day's reading will focus on the key verse to memorize for the week. In the other weekly readings, you will be invited to read a passage from Ephesians, reflect on the text, and then respond with some guided journal questions. On the final day, you will review the key verse again and recite it from memory. As you work through the six weeks' worth of material in this section, you will read (and, in some cases, reread) the entire book of Ephesians.

Now, you may be wondering why you will be doing this over the course of *forty* days. Certainly, there is nothing special about that number. But there is something biblical about it. In Scripture, the number forty typically designates a time of *testing*. The great flood in Noah's time lasted forty days. Moses lived forty years in Egypt and another forty years in the desert before he led God's people. He spent forty days on Mount Sinai receiving God's laws and sent spies, for forty days, to investigate the land of Canaan. Later, God sent the prophet Jonah to warn ancient Nineveh, for forty days, that its destruction would come because of the people's sins.

Even more critically, in the New Testament we read that Jesus spent forty days in the wilderness, fasting and praying. It marked a critical transition point in his ministry—the place where he set about to fulfill the mission that God had intended. During this time Jesus was tested relentlessly by the enemy . . . and prevailed. When he returned to Galilee, he was a different person than the man who had entered into the wilderness forty days before. The same will be true for you as you commit to this forty-day journey through Ephesians.

GROUP FACILITATION

You and your fellow group members should have your own copy of this study guide. Not only will this help you engage when your group is meeting, but it will also allow you to fully enter into the *40 Days* learning experience. Keep in mind the video, questions, and activities are simply tools to help you engage with the session. The real power and life-transformation will come as you dig into the Scriptures and seek to live out the truths you learn along the way.

Finally, you will need to appoint a leader or facilitator for the group who is responsible for starting the video teaching and for keeping track of time during discussions and activities. Leaders may also read questions aloud and monitor discussions, prompting participants to respond and ensuring that everyone has the opportunity to participate. For more thorough instructions on this role, see the Leader's Guide included at the back of this guide.

EPHESIANS

AUTHOR, DATE, AND LOCATION

The apostle Paul wrote this letter to the church in Ephesus c. AD 60–62. At the time, he was under house arrest, chained to a Roman solider twenty-four hours a day. He had few freedoms as a prisoner of Rome, but he was allowed to have guests and also write letters to some of the churches that he cared deeply about. One of those churches was a congregation in the city of Ephesus (in modern-day Turkey), where Paul had spent more than two years. One of the things the apostle celebrated was that this congregation looked like the vision of heaven that we see in the book of Revelation (see 7:9). It was a multiethnic, beautifully diverse body of men and women, Jews and Gentiles, enslaved and free people. The people in the Ephesian church were from a wide variety of tribes, people groups, and nations. On top of all this, they loved each other! They were united in Jesus. Their community not only embraced the gospel but also showed the world what that gospel could look like.

THE BIG PICTURE

Ephesus was filled with pagan temples, and idolatry was rampant. There was tension between Jews and Gentiles (non-Jews) that had been brewing off and on for centuries. The Jewish people held the Gentiles in contempt for mistreating their people throughout their history. The Gentiles held the Jews in contempt for seeing them as immoral and "unclean." How were these two radically diverse groups of people going to become a loving and united family? It looked impossible from a human perspective. But Ephesians is a reminder that God loves taking what looks impossible and turning it upside-down. Our God can take enemies and make them friends. He can take people from every walk of life and help them walk in the unity of his Son.

The six chapters of Ephesians can be seen as two movements in the same story of God seeking to build a multiethnic, united, loving family of dramatically diverse people. Both sections address the same topics but in different ways. Movement one, the first three chapters of Ephesians, is about *who we are in Christ*. Paul looks at our identity as followers of Jesus and lays out more than twenty distinct and powerful pictures for us to lock into our heart and soul. When we know who God is and who we are, we have a fresh outlook on the people around us. We can see them as God does.

Movement two, chapters four through six of Ephesians, are about *how we live in Christ*. The apostle Paul communicates more than thirty commands and directives for ways that God's diverse family members need to live in community. If we are going to be a race of grace, we must walk in the ways of Jesus, put off old patterns and behaviors, and love others as Jesus does. When we know who we are and when we have deep conviction about who God is, then we know how to live, love, serve, and grow in community with other people.

The truth and power of Ephesians leaves a tattoo on our souls. God's plan is bigger than just us and Jesus. His vision is as big as the world and as dynamic as the people he has made. When we realize that the grace of Jesus is big enough for everyone—even people who are different than us—we can become part of God's plan to build his diverse family of faith.

EPIC THEMES

There are many themes in Ephesians that are worthy of our focus. Some of these include:

- **Jesus loves his diverse family.** Grace is the pathway into God's family. God is drawing in people from every tribe, background, and walk of life, and his family is always as diverse as the human race. Jesus is Lord and the Holy Spirit transforms hearts, so God's family can be united and love one another in the midst of many differences. When this happens, God delights, and the world looks on in wonder (see Ephesians 1:1–10).

- **We are chosen and marked.** God has a plan and a purpose. His gospel is the source of salvation and the transformation that every person needs. By his Holy Spirit he draws us, marks us, and leads us (see Ephesians 1:11–14).

- **God is making a new race of grace.** God is making a family of people from every nation and background. All are invited into God's race of grace and united to each other. It is a shocking vision of God's power to save, heal, and bind people into a community (see Ephesians 1:15–2:13).

- **God delights when his family lives at peace with others.** The peace that Paul writes about is not a cessation of turmoil or tension. It is a picture of people walking with Jesus toward each other and becoming a family. It was no easy task for Jews and Gentiles to live in peace and become a model of unity for the world. But, in the power of Jesus, it became a reality in the church in Ephesus—and it can be a reality in the church today (see Ephesians 2:14–22).

- **We are servants of the gospel.** Everyone will end up serving someone or something. Followers of Jesus learn that serving the gospel, sharing it with the world, and being a model of the transforming power of Jesus is the absolute best investment of our lives (see Ephesians 3:1–21).

- **We are called to a new life.** Followers of Jesus are called to strip off the old ways and take on the heart of Jesus. Out with impurity, greed, obscenity, and in with humility, patience, love, and thankfulness. As we allow Jesus to shape our lives, his family becomes healthy, vibrant, and shines the light of the gospel in our dark world (see Ephesians 4:1–6:9).

- **We are called to stand strong.** There is a battle at hand. Our awareness of that battle does not change the reality of it one single bit! There are dark forces of evil at work in the heavenly realms, and every person in God's family needs to stand, put on the armor of the Spirit, and fight back. When we do, we will see the victory of Jesus (see Ephesians 6:10–24).

In a world of division, conflict, and polarization, the same Jesus who united the Jews and Gentiles, enslaved and free people, men and women, and people from every tribe and tongue some 2,000 years ago in Ephesus, is ready to do it again. God is still building his diverse family of faith. It will not always be easy, but when we participate and partner with God in his plans, we bring him glory, bless other believers, and serve as a witness to the world.

A REVOLUTIONARY IDEA

EPHESIANS 1:1–23

Of all the revolutionary ideas found in the Bible, one that should shake us and wake us up is that God turns enemies into friends and is uniting people of radically diverse backgrounds into one beautiful and loving family.

WELCOME

The Bible is full of revolutionary ideas. This should not surprise us. From the first word of Genesis to the final word of Revelation, the Creator and Sustainer of the universe is speaking. He is sovereign, all-powerful, glorious, and his ways are not our ways. When God spoke at the beginning of all things, the heavens, the earth, and all of creation sprung into existence out of nothing (see Genesis 1–2). This is stunning beyond description. One day the Spirit and the bride will say, "Come" and all of history will be rolled up like a scroll (Revelation 22:17). Amazing!

Sometimes we read the words of God contained in the pages of the Bible and forget how counter-cultural and shocking they were at the time they were written—and how shocking they still are today. Instead of being amazed, we pass over these ideas as if they are common. Because they are familiar, we forget that they are revolutionary.

Jesus said, "Love your enemies and pray for those who persecute you" (Matthew 5:44). This call runs counter to our human nature and is as shocking today as it was when Christ declared it some 2,000 years ago. John wrote, "For God so loved the world that he gave his one and only Son" (John 3:16). What depth of love could have moved the Father to offer his precious Son for us? James wrote, "Humble yourselves before the Lord, and he will lift you up" (James 4:10). God's call for each of us is to put aside our own personal pride and look first to the needs of others. These words are revolutionary in the culture of our day.

We find these similar staggering words in the opening of Paul's letter to the Ephesians: "For he chose us in him before the creation of the world to be holy and blameless in his sight. In love he predestined us for adoption to sonship through Jesus Christ . . . he made known to us the mystery of his will according to his good pleasure, which he purposed in Christ, to be put into effect when the times reach their fulfillment—to *bring unity to all things* in heaven and on earth under Christ" (1:4–5, 8–10, emphasis added).

God chose before the foundation of the world and adopted us into his own family. The Almighty Creator has made known to us the mystery of his will. And he desires to bring unity to all things under Christ. He is birthing a family of diverse people who will be a loving and united family today and forever. This vision bears the seeds of heavenly revolution!

SHARE

Think about what it would look like if local Christian congregations became a picture of beautiful diversity and radical unity. What message would this send to the world around us? What would onlookers learn about our God just by looking at us?

WATCH

Play the video segment for session one (see the streaming video access provided on the inside front cover). As you watch, use the following outline to record any thoughts or concepts that stand out to you.

Churches in the first century were trans-cultural and were socially, economically, and racially diverse

The precious blood of Jesus not only forgives sins but also unleashes the heavenly power needed to create a family out of people from every tribe, people group, and nation

Separate ingredients or a wonderful salad—which will it be?

All people (Jews and Gentiles) can be reconciled vertically to God and horizontally to each other through Jesus

The grace of Jesus creates a new and diverse family that is blessed beyond description (Ephesians 1:1–6)

God makes enemies into family through the redemption offered in the blood of Jesus (Ephesians 1:7–10)

God turns enemies into friends by sealing us with his love in the power of the Holy Spirit (Ephesians 1:11–14)

God turns enemies into a loving family when we keep our eyes firmly fixed on Jesus (Ephesians 1:15–23)

DISCUSS

Take a few minutes with your group members to discuss what you just watched and explore these concepts in Scripture. Use the following questions to help guide your discussion.

1. What impacted you the most as you watched Derwin's teaching?

2. What are ways that churches today are taking Jesus-honoring steps forward in embracing diversity in the family of God? Why is it important that we continue making this a priority in the life of the church?

3. How is the Church made more beautiful, strong, and effective when we view it more like a salad than just the individual ingredients that make up the salad? What do we miss out on if we don't celebrate and embrace our differences?

4. **Read Ephesians 1:1–6.** What are some of the blessings God brings into our lives and his church when we learn to walk in unity? How have you personally experienced one of these blessings?

5. **Read Ephesians 1:7–10.** Of what are we set free through the blood of Jesus? How should this transform the way we live as individual Christians and as the family of God?

6. **Read Ephesians 1:11–14.** When we are sealed by the Holy Spirit and filled with the Spirit, we experience power for transformation. How have you experienced the Holy Spirit doing one of these things in your life:

- Helping you follow God's purpose and live in his will?
- Helping you live with confident and growing hope?
- Letting your life bring praise and glory to God?
- Empowering you to walk in unity with believers who are different than you?
- Helping you live with awareness of the heavenly inheritance that is yours?

How can your group members specifically pray for you as you seek to grow in one of the areas listed above?

MEMORIZE

Each session, you will be given a key verse (or verses) from the passage covered in the video teaching to memorize. This week, your memory verse is from Ephesians 1:3:

Praise be to the God and Father of our Lord Jesus Christ, who has blessed us in the heavenly realms with every spiritual blessing in Christ.

Have everyone recite this verse out loud. Then go around the room and ask for any volunteers who would like to say the verse from memory.

RESPOND

What will you take away from this session? What is one practical next step you can take to walk in harmony and unity with Christians who are different that you?

PRAY

Close your group time by praying in any of the following directions:

- Thank God for the wonderful diversity in his people (and Church) all over your community, nation, and the world. Lift up praise for specific ways God has made people unique and beautiful.
- Confess where you have been fearful or resistant to embrace believers from different tongues, tribes, nations, and backgrounds.
- Pray for unity in your church, the churches in your community, and in the body of Christ around the world. Ask God to use the unity of his people to be a shining light in our dark world.

SESSION ONE

Reflect on the material you have covered in this session by engaging in the following between-session learning resources. Each week, you will begin by reviewing the key verse(s) to memorize for the session. During the next five days, you will have an opportunity to read a portion of Ephesians, reflect on what you learn, respond by taking action, journal some of your insights, and pray about what God has taught you. Finally, on the last day, you will review the theme of the session, reflect on what you have learned, and review how it has impacted your life.

DAY 1

Memorize: Begin this week's personal study by reciting Ephesians 1:3:

> *Praise be to the God and Father of our Lord Jesus Christ, who has blessed us in the heavenly realms with every spiritual blessing in Christ.*

Now try to say the verse completely from memory.

Reflect: Let those words wash over your soul and expand your mind. Through faith in Jesus, you now have at your disposal "every spiritual blessing." Full and complete forgiveness of your sins . . . *check!* The fruit of the Holy Spirit growing in you . . . *check!* Heaven as your home . . . *check!* The family of God, the Church, as a haven in this lonely world . . . *check!* The list goes on and on. What are some of the spiritual blessings God has given you? Ponder them, write them below, reflect on good gifts, and seek to live with a growing awareness of "every spiritual blessing." Lift up a prayer of thanks to Jesus for making all this possible.

DAY 2

Read: Ephesians 1:1–10.

Reflect: You have been adopted into the family of God. We all have been—if we have placed our faith in Jesus. This puts us on equal footing before the cross, in the heart of God, and in his Church. Every one of us should lift our voices in praise and bow our knees in adoration. One reason we should live and walk in absolute unity in the family of God is that God saw fit to adopt us as his daughters and sons. Like a beautiful tapestry, God is weaving together people of every imaginable background and making us one. Why is it so important that we learn to see every believer—including ourselves—as invited guests in God's family?

Journal:

- What potential problems might we experience in the Church if we see ourselves as "natural born members" of God's family who have a special place but look at other people in the Church as adopted guests?
- God is seeking to bring unity all over our divided earth, and one way he accomplishes this is through the examples of Christians and churches who live and walk in unity. What are simple steps of unity you can take in the flow of a normal day?

Pray: Ask God to show you where your attitudes, behaviors, or words might be causing division or disunity in the church and confess these patterns. Pray for the Holy Spirit to work in you and through you to bring unity in your home, friendships, and the Church.

DAY 3

Read: Ephesians 1:11–12.

Reflect: God has a plan. He moves with divine purpose. Our creator does not act in random ways. He chooses and moves in ways that will accomplish his divine will. The end result is always his glory. When our world feels out of control, when conflicts arise, when our own weakness gets the best of us, we can turn our eyes to heaven and know that the Maker of all things is still on the throne and is in the process of working all things for the praise of his glory. How can you turn your eyes to heaven when life gets crazy and feels out of control?

Journal:
- How has God surprised you in the past by showing up, delivering, protecting, or leading you in difficult times? Write down one or two specific times you looked back and recognized that God was in control even when things seemed chaotic.
- What are you facing today that feels like it is spinning and veering off course? How can remembering God's

sovereign presence and movement in the past help you stand strong in your faith as you face this situation in the present?

Pray: Invite God to bring to your mind and heart different times in the past when he has guided, protected, or led you through hard times. Lift up thanks for his sovereign power being unleashed in your life and pray for your eyes to see his presence with you today.

DAY 4

Read: Ephesians 1:13–14.

Reflect: In the ancient world, letters were closed with a seal. Hot wax was poured to close the letter and make it secure, and then a signet ring or stamp was pressed into the wax as it cooled. The imprint of the seal showed who it was from. It was like a signature on an email. When we placed our faith in Jesus, the Holy Spirit of the living God fell on us, moved into us, and placed his seal on our heart. We are his. He watches over us. Every follower of Jesus bears this seal. It is one of the things that unites us and makes us one. What are signs that the Holy Spirit of God has moved into your life and marked your heart with his presence?

Journal:
- When you first placed your faith in Jesus, how did you experience the Holy Spirit of God moving into your life and placing a seal on your heart?
- What inheritance have you already received from God? What are you promised to receive when you see him face to face one day?

Pray: Thank the Father for sealing you with the Holy Spirit and ask for the power of the Spirit to help you live each day for the praise of God's glory.

DAY 5

Read: Ephesians 1:15–18.

Reflect: When we know we are adopted, loved, and sealed by the Spirit of God, it should move us to pray with fresh vigor for other believers. This is what the apostle Paul did. He could not stop giving thanks for God's people in the church at Ephesus. They were in his heart, on his lips, and lifted up. He could not stop praying for them! How should we pray for the beautiful and diverse family of God? What does the apostle Paul model in his joy-filled prayer?

Journal:
- What specific prayers does Paul lift up in Ephesians 1:16–18? How can you make these prayers your prayer as you lift up other Christians you know?
- How can you make each of the prayers modeled by Paul a universal prayer for all Christians around the world?

Pray: Pray for believers around the world to know the riches of God's glorious inheritance. Pray that they will recognize one of these great gifts is the spiritual reality that the diverse people of God are one united family.

DAY 6

Read: Ephesians 1:19–23.

Reflect: Let the truth of this passage sink into your soul. The mighty power of God that raised Jesus from the dead and conquered sin and hell is in you! Jesus rules and reigns over the entire universe and over your life. He rules through all history and for eternity. He is the head over all things for the sake of his Church, the family of God. Where do you tend to look for strength and energy when you feel depleted? What does this passage say about God's power?

Journal:
- What situations sap your energy? What are ways you can look to Jesus, rely on your Savior, and draw strength from his endless reserve of heavenly power?
- One of the ways God empowers us is through the community of his diverse and global family. Who are people in the church who bring you encouragement? How can you connect with them in ways that will empower you and them?

Pray: Praise God for the power he has to rule and reign over all things. Ask him to fill you with the strength you need in any areas you are feeling empty and in need of divine strength.

DAY 7

Memorize: Conclude this week's personal study by again reciting Ephesians 1:3:

> *Praise be to the God and Father of our Lord Jesus Christ, who has blessed us in the heavenly realms with every spiritual blessing in Christ.*

Now try to say the verse completely from memory.

Reflect: The source of the spiritual blessings that God lavishes on us is found in Jesus. As we walk with him, grow in faith, love him more, and share his good news with others, we experience his blessings. What are ways you can go deeper in your relationship with Jesus in the coming week? How can you make time to sit at his feet, reflect on his Word, and share his love? As you are in Christ, you experience the spiritual blessings he has prepared for you.

A NEW RACE OF GRACE

EPHESIANS 2:1–13

Our broken world and our sinful hearts have a way of dividing people in ever-increasing ways. Jesus came to unite people into one beautiful family, and he has called us to join him on this mission of forming a new race of grace.

WELCOME

Sin drives us toward division. Without Jesus we are doomed to fight, hate, resent, and live in conflict with those who are different than us (and even with those who are very similar). When Jesus entered human history, he saw the divisions that were ravaging his beloved creation.

The Jews hated Gentiles, and the Gentiles hated them right back. This caused racial and ethnic divisions that seemed insurmountable. Men and women were seen as radically different, and this caused gender-based conflict continually. Many people in the world were bound in slavery, and this deep sin created two classes of people—the free and the captive. This economic and class separation had ripped people apart. One of the reasons Jesus came was to restore people to right relationships and do away with these divisions.

Jesus came to tear down the dividing wall of hostility and make people one. His vision was a loving family where Jews and Gentiles, men and women, enslaved and free, were all living on an equal footing. Jesus came to make enemies friends. He lived to make us alive to his grace and dead to our sinful past. He died to give us life in his forever family where people from every tongue, tribe, nation, and background could live in heavenly harmony right here on earth.

In a time when polarization and division seem to be increasing, the only hope for our hearts, homes, and world is the One who gave his life as a perfect sacrifice to make us children of God. When this happens and we become part of God's family, there is hope for unity, common love, and a dismantling of all the divisions that keep us at war with other people.

SHARE

How are you seeing divisions and conflict growing between groups of people? What is one example you have seen of Jesus bringing unity where no one else could?

WATCH

Play the video segment for session two (see the streaming video access provided on the inside front cover). As you watch, use the following outline to record any thoughts or concepts that stand out to you.

The reality of spiritual deadness . . . Jesus did not come to make bad people good; he came to make dead people alive (Ephesians 2:1–2 and Genesis 3)

Our spiritual reality should lead to deep humility (Ephesians 2:3)

"But God . . . " Embracing God's free love and mercy (Ephesians 2:4–5)

We are made alive by Christ, and we now live in Christ (Ephesians 2:5)

We are a new race of grace (Ephesians 2:6–7)

The amazing gift of grace and the reality of who we are—
God's trophies (Ephesians 2:8–10)

How people who are exiles, separate, and excluded become
part of God's beautiful and diverse family (Ephesians 2:11–13)

God's plan was never to meet our self-designed expectations
but to sweep us into his divine story

DISCUSS

Take a few minutes with your group members to discuss what
you just watched and explore these concepts in Scripture. Use
the following questions to help guide your discussion.

1. What impacted you the most as you watched Derwin's teaching?

2. **Read Ephesians 2:1–3.** When did you move from being spiritually dead to being alive in Jesus? How did your life change? If you are not yet a follower of Jesus, what is keeping you from taking the step of placing your faith in him?

3. **Read Ephesians 2:4–5.** How has God shown us his love and mercy through the life and sacrifice of Jesus? How is he still revealing his love and mercy to us today?

4. **Read Ephesians 2:5–7.** Every person who has put faith in Jesus will be with him in heaven someday. What is amazing is that we are "in Christ" today! What does it mean to be alive in Christ and to live each moment in Christ today? How does this spiritual reality impact your life in the flow of a normal day?

5. **Read Ephesians 2:8–10.** What does it mean to see ourselves as God's trophies? How could our outlook on the Church be transformed if we saw every person from every background and ethnicity as a trophy of God's amazing grace?

6. Jesus has been restoring people to unity and harmony throughout history. He has the power to heal the brokenness between Jews and Gentiles, men and women, and every human division we can imagine. What are some practical ways you can join God on this amazing journey of reconciliation and healing between divided groups of people?

MEMORIZE

Your memory verses this week are from Ephesians 2:4–5:

But because of his great love for us, God, who is rich in mercy, made us alive with Christ even when we were dead in transgressions—it is by grace you have been saved.

Have everyone recite these verses out loud. Then ask for any volunteers who would like to say the verses from memory.

RESPOND

What will you take away from this session? What is one practical next step you can take to celebrate the unity we find in Jesus and to grow harmony between you and people who are different than you (in the eyes of the world)?

PRAY

Close your group time by praying in any of the following directions:

- Thank Jesus for his amazing sacrifice and example of loving people from every possible background with equal grace and care. Be sure to thank him for loving you with infinite grace.
- Confess where you have let conflict arise in your life or where you have treated others unfairly or poorly simply because they seem different than you. (Some may want to pray silently and others out loud. Be sure to leave time for silent prayer and don't rush past this time.)
- Pray for the power that God provides for you, your church, and God's people worldwide to resist the temptation to divide and treat people poorly (or better) because of their differences. Ask God for wisdom as you seek to love people, embrace them, and live as family with those who are not like you.

SESSION TWO

Reflect on the material you have covered in this session by engaging in the following between-session learning resources. Each week, you will begin by reviewing the key verse(s) to memorize for the session. During the next five days, you will have an opportunity to read a portion of Ephesians, reflect on what you learn, respond by taking action, journal some of your insights, and pray about what God has taught you. Finally, on the last day, you will review the key verse(s) and reflect on what you have learned for the week.

DAY 8

Memorize: Begin this week's personal study by reciting Ephesians 2:4–5:

> *But because of his great love for us, God, who is rich in mercy, made us alive with Christ even when we were dead in transgressions—it is by grace you have been saved.*

Now try to say these verses completely from memory.

Reflect: We were made alive with Christ, even though we were dead in sin, because Jesus gave his life for us. We were far away, and he brought us near . . . we did not find our way home! Jesus paid the price for a one-way ticket back to the heart of God and into his family. We did not find peace in ourselves or our good works. Jesus became our peace and gave us his peace. Why is it essential that we recognize that our salvation and the peace we experience are gifts of grace from Jesus and not prizes we won by our good works?

DAY 9

Read: Ephesians 2:1–3.

Reflect: We can fool others and hide the truth from family and friends, but God knows our heart and our history. Our Creator knew what was hidden in every closet of our past and forgotten in the darkness of our heart—and he still loved us. He knew our fleshly cravings and earthly desires that deserved eternal judgment and paid the price to wash it all away. Jesus came to crush the head of the serpent and to set us free. What has Jesus' grace done for you? What has he removed? How has his sacrifice delivered you from the wrath you deserved?

Journal:

- What praise can you lift to the God who loved you when you were saturated in sin?
- Who are people you know who are still living in their transgressions? How can you pray for them and show them the amazing grace that Jesus is ready to offer?

Pray: Lift up praise after praise for the cleansing and deliverance that Jesus gave freely to you.

DAY 10

Read: Ephesians 2:4–5.

Reflect: Jesus did not come to make bad people good. He came to make dead people alive. By his grace, we can do good works that please him, but his mission was to breathe life into our dead spirits and bring new birth. Our transgressions killed us, eternally. His grace brings to life, eternally. Pause right now, take a deep breath, and then slowly release it. As you do, thank your loving Savior that you are now born again by grace and ask him to help you live this new life for the sake of his glory. What will help you walk through each day with a new and fresh awareness that you are alive in the power and grace of Jesus?

Journal:
- What were parts of you (dreams, relationships, hopes, and other things) that were dead and are now alive? What are signs that you are alive in Jesus?
- What are areas of your life that might still be dwelling in darkness and need the light of Jesus to become fully alive? What step can you take to expose one specific area to the light, grace, and power of Jesus?

Pray: Ask for power to live each and every day with a profound and unbending conviction that you live and breathe, every moment, because of the grace of Jesus.

DAY 11

Read: Ephesians 2:6–7.

Reflect: We dwell in the heavenly realms now and forever! Yes, our address is still on this earth with all of its challenges and struggles, but our home is in heaven. We have been raised up. We are seated with Christ in the heavenly realms. In the coming ages, and forever more, we will dwell with Jesus in glory. But today, the spiritual reality is undeniable—we dwell with Jesus, and he lives in us. How might the choices you make and things you do tomorrow change if you were fully aware that you dwell with Jesus and he lives fully in you . . . right now?

Journal:
- What do you have planned for tomorrow? How can you get ready to live in a new way because you are reminded that Jesus will be with you every moment of the day?
- What are some of the heavenly blessings that you will not fully experience and understand until this life ends and you are face-to-face with Jesus?

Pray: Thank Jesus for the unimaginable and incomprehensible riches that await you in heaven and pray for daily awareness of the hope that awaits you one day.

DAY 12

Read: Ephesians 2:8–10.

Reflect: We are saved by grace and not by works. The works we do have no power to save us. But because we are saved, we can't help but to do them! We must never mix up the order of these two things. Our works have no power to pressure God to extend grace to us. His grace came when we did not deserve it, because we never could earn it. But when we are lavished by God's grace and recognize his goodness, we respond by living for him. Our attitudes change and we do good things by his power. God actually prepares and leads us to do good for his glory. Our good works are always a response to his grace. Why do you think so many people get this mixed up and believe they must do good things to earn God's grace and love?

Journal:
- What are ways you are experiencing God's grace in this season of your life?

- How can you respond to God's goodness, love, and grace by doing good things in his power and for his glory? When will you act on this invitation to good works?

Pray: Ask Jesus to help you keep focused on grace so that you can respond with good works. Confess where you sometimes get these things mixed up and try to earn his favor by your actions and good deeds.

DAY 13

Read: Ephesians 2:11–13.

Reflect: You were separated, excluded, and a foreigner to God's promises. Your sin was a chasm greater than the Grand Canyon. There was no way you could deal with it, remove it, or jump over it. You were powerless and hopeless. But then Jesus showed up, and his undeserved and infinite goodness came crashing onto the shore of your heart and washed over you. Through his sacrifice, you were cleansed and engrafted into his diverse family. Do you remember the feeling that came over you when you first experienced the greatness of God's grace?

Journal:

- How did Jesus reveal his grace and love for you? Who did he use to show it?
- How has God's grace changed you and freed you?

Pray: Spend time thanking God, from the depth of your heart, for all of his amazing and transforming grace.

DAY 14

Memorize: Conclude this week's personal study by again reciting Ephesians 2:4–5:

> *But because of his great love for us, God, who is rich in mercy, made us alive with Christ even when we were dead in transgressions—it is by grace you have been saved.*

Now try to say these verses completely from memory.

Reflect: Our world does a lot of excluding and dividing. Jesus is about uniting and building a diverse and beautiful family where his grace, love, and peace prevail. We were far away from

Jesus, from heaven, from other people, from peace, from the family we all long to experience. All that is good and beautiful was out of our reach! Then Jesus, in his amazing grace, made us alive. What has Jesus provided for you that you could never have gotten on your own? How can you delight in these gifts and give him praise for his love?

A FAMILY OF PEACE

EPHESIANS 2:14–22

When God's diverse community is healthy, peace marks our relationship with God, with others in the Church, and with the world around us. Because of the grace and sacrifice of Jesus, we can become his agents of reconciliation, justice, and love in our broken and divided world.

WELCOME

Imagine a married couple who delight in each other, speak well of one another (even when their spouse is not around), and openly honor and serve one another. This would get people's attention. An example like this would be a beacon of hope to so many people who long for a peaceful and harmonious marriage—and wonder if it is even possible.

Imagine a leader in a community who is compassionate with the hurting and honest in all of his or her dealings. This person's word is his or her bond, and everyone knows this individual is quick to listen, careful with words, and committed to stand behind what is promised. This would lead to trust and confidence in the hearts of those in that community.

Now imagine a local church filled with Christians who are examples of peace. They know God and are at rest because they are confident that Jesus has washed their sins away. They not only have peace with God but also love and trust each other. The members model peace in their relationships with the other members of their uniquely diverse congregation. But they don't stop there. These people seek peace with those outside their church. They strive for justice. They include the broken, outcast, forgotten, with open hearts and arms. Everywhere these Jesus followers go, they bring peace—and the people they meet can feel it.

What kind of witness would this bring to the world? What would it reveal about Jesus? How would it attract people to the beautiful and diverse family of God called the Church? Now imagine there where tens of thousands of these Jesus communities seeking peace all over the world. As Paul reveals this section of Ephesians, this is exactly what God desires!

SHARE

Talk about one way the church you attend seeks to be an agent of peace in your community. Describe how this reveals the presence and love of Jesus to the world.

WATCH

Play the video segment for session three (see the streaming video access provided on the inside front cover). As you watch, use the following outline to record any thoughts or concepts that stand out to you.

Paul—when a divider becomes a uniter and agent of peace

An important mark of God's diverse family . . . peace!

In the grace of Jesus, we have vertical peace with God so we can be a model of peace in a turmoil-filled world (Ephesians 2:13–15)

Jesus brings us horizontal peace with the people around us inside and outside of the Church (Ephesians 2:15–18).

Is your cross too small? Then make it bigger!

Our Father has no favorites because we are all his favorites
(Matthew 5:7, 9; Ephesians 2:19)

Don't rebuild walls that Jesus died to tear down
(Ephesians 2:14, 19–21)

Let lament and worship propel you forward as a peacemaker
(Ephesians 2:19–22)

DISCUSS

Take a few minutes with your group members to discuss what
you just watched and explore these concepts in Scripture. Use
the following questions to help guide your discussion.

1. What impacted you the most as you watched Derwin's teaching?

2. **Read Ephesians 2:14.** What are signs that our world is chaotic and in need of peace in our homes, communities, churches, government, and world at large? How can we partner with Jesus to bring peace in these areas of life?

3. **Read Ephesians 2:13–14.** What is most important about any Christian is not his or her skin color, gender, political affiliation, economic status, or any other human standard. What matters most is that we are *in Christ* and gripped by his amazing grace. What are some possible dangers if we make something else the primary focal point of who we believe we are? How can our lives be more peace-filled when we live with bold confidence that what matters most about us is being united with Jesus?

4. **Read Ephesians 2:15–19.** Having peace with God establishes a vertical relationship that transforms our life. When this is secure, we can also find peace on a horizontal level with the people around us. How will we treat others if we see them as loved children of God whom Jesus died to save?

What can you do to increase harmony and peace between you and people you know who are still far away from God?

5. **Read Ephesians 2:20–22.** Jesus came to tear down walls between people, but we often seek to build walls that separate us from others. How can *authentic faith*, *confident hope* in Jesus, and *passionate love* for others tear down walls of division and differences? Share an example of a wall torn down by faith, hope, or love.

6. Our world is longing for peace! How can sharing the peace we have found in Jesus help draw those who are resistant to faith or cynical about Christianity? How have you discovered peace with Jesus and with others because of your faith in Jesus?

MEMORIZE

Your memory verse this week is from Ephesians 2:14:

For he himself is our peace, who has made the two groups one and has destroyed the barrier, the dividing wall of hostility.

Have everyone recite this verse out loud. Then ask for any volunteers who would like to say the verse from memory.

RESPOND

What will you take away from this session? What is one practical next step you can take to be a person who better seeks peace, reconciliation, and justice?

PRAY

Close your group time by praying in any of the following directions:

- Thank God for sending Jesus to lay down his life so we could receive his peace and be restored in our relationship with him and with the people in our life.
- Ask for courage and power to stand against injustice, racism, and things that drive people apart and away from Jesus.
- Pray for your church, home, and life to become havens of peace that draw people closer to Jesus in our conflicted and peace-starved world.

SESSION THREE

Reflect on the material you have covered in this session by engaging in the following between-session learning resources. Each week, you will begin by reviewing the key verse(s) to memorize for the session. During the next five days, you will have an opportunity to read a portion of Ephesians and reflect on what you learn, respond by taking action, journal some of your insights, and pray about what God has taught you. Finally, on the last day, you will review the key verse(s) and reflect on what you have learned for the week.

DAY 15

Memorize: Begin this week's personal study by reciting Ephesians 2:14:

> *For he himself is our peace, who has made the two groups one and has destroyed the barrier, the dividing wall of hostility.*

Now try to say the verse completely from memory.

Reflect: Jesus is a uniter! He brought together the most embattled and embittered groups of people in his day. He still loves to do this. Think about some of the most polarized and conflicted situations in your community and world. Now pause and reflect on the fact that Jesus has the power to unite these people and bring them lasting peace. As a matter of fact, he is the *only one* who can bring lasting and eternal peace to conflicted people and situations. How can you pray for peace and be an agent of God's peace right where he has placed you?

DAY 16

Read: Ephesians 2:14–15.

Reflect: What walls stand between you and other people? Walls of fear? Walls of distrust? Walls of jealousy? Walls of apathy? Walls of unforgiveness? The list of walls is as vast as human sin and the enemy's lies. Remember that Jesus came to tear down the walls between us and God and the walls that have been built between us and other people. What can you do to tear down one wall today? Start there. Then work on another.

Journal:
- What are some of the walls you tend to build between yourself and the people Jesus loves and cares about? What does Jesus think about these walls?
- What are specific ways you can identify your wall-building attitudes and actions and stop before you build another wall?

Pray: Pray for eyes to see the walls in your life, for courage to name them, and for strength (with Jesus) to tear them down.

DAY 17

Read: Ephesians 2:16.

Reflect: Jesus left the glory of heaven and came to our world to reconcile us to God. He came to make us a part of his family—a new race of grace? This happens when we come to the cross, confess our sins, and receive God's grace. In the light of God's glory and kindness, our hostility toward others then begins to die. Walls fall and community grows. How have your relationships become more loving, grace-filled, and less hostile since you placed your faith in Jesus?

Journal:

- What are some of the ways that God has removed hostility and conflict from your relationships because you have been reconciled to Jesus?
- Where is there still conflict and tension in your relational world? What can you do to partner with Jesus in putting an end to this hostility?

Pray: Thank Jesus for reconciling people to himself (including you) and pray for the strength you need to be an agent of relational healing and reconciliation everywhere you go.

DAY 18

Read: Ephesians 2:17–18.

Reflect: Jesus preached peace to those who were near (the Jewish people) and those who were far (the Gentiles). Our Savior and Good Shepherd still offers his peace to all people. Anyone who will listen and humbly receive his message of grace can have access to a healed and loving relationship with their heavenly Father. The Holy Spirit is working right now, calling people to come home. How are you being an instrument of that peace that Jesus came to bring?

Journal:
- Who are people you care about who do not yet have a saving friendship with Jesus? What is standing in the way of them hearing and receiving God's offer of grace?
- What are ways you can partner with the Spirit of the Living God to help each of these people see Jesus more clearly and hear his invitation to come home to their Father?

Pray: Praise the Father for making access to salvation. Thank Jesus for paying the price and offering his life for your sins. Invite the Holy Spirit to empower you to boldly and wisely share the hope and grace that only God can bring to each lost and wandering person.

DAY 19

Read: Ephesians 2:19.

Reflect: In this world, some people feel like insiders and some feel like outsiders. But the reality is that we *all* are foreigners and strangers to God because sin has driven us away from our spiritual home. God's desire is to bring us back. He wants us to live as citizens of his kingdom and members of his family. We do not need to live separated from God and far away from his grace. He offers an invitation to *every* human being who will accept it. What helped you recognize your need for Jesus and his loving invitation to come to the Father through faith in him?

Journal:

- What does it mean to be a full-fledged citizen of God's kingdom? What privileges does this citizenship bring?
- God calls you a member of his household—you are part of his forever family. How does this truth bring hope and a sense of belonging in your world?

Pray: Give God praise for making you a citizen of his kingdom and a loved member of his family. Pray that people in our world who feel unworthy of belonging will discover that the God who made them longs to see them come home to his grace.

DAY 20

Read: Ephesians 2:20–22.

Reflect: In the ancient world where the Scriptures were written, many of the homes were built with stones and not wood. Rocks were plentiful and trees were scarce. When a mason or carpenter would prepare to build a house, they would first fashion and place a cornerstone. If it was perfectly shaped, the walls of the house would be true and the corners square. The house would be solid and stand. As followers of Jesus, when we build our lives based on him, we will stand strong. When he is our cornerstone, we are built into a holy temple for his glory. What can you do, on a daily basis, to be sure you are building your life on the cornerstone of Jesus?

Journal:
- What habits and life-patterns do you have in place to keep you building your life on the foundation and cornerstone of Jesus? How can you develop these even more?
- What are some new life patterns you can develop that will help you to build all you are and all you do on Jesus?

Pray: Thank Jesus for being your cornerstone and pray for the Holy Spirit's power to help you build on him (and only him) each day of your life.

DAY 21

Memorize: Conclude this week's personal study by again reciting Ephesians 2:14:

> *For he himself is our peace, who has made the two groups one and has destroyed the barrier, the dividing wall of hostility.*

Reflect: Jesus came to destroy barriers and tear down the walls that separate people. When we find peace with him (vertical peace), we can then walk in peace with the people around us (horizontal peace). When this happens, God can use us to tear down dividing walls of injustice. What are some of the injustices you see around you? What is your next step to tear down a dividing wall that you or someone else has erected between people?

SERVANTS OF THE GOSPEL

EPHESIANS 3:1–21

When we live as servants of Jesus and follow his world-transforming ways, we build a beautiful and diverse community marked by prayer, love, and unity that reveal the presence and person of Jesus to our world.

WELCOME

Sometimes we miss the greatness of something when it is in front of us day after day. It becomes so familiar that we fail to recognize its impact, grandeur, and size. Just think about the sun that warms our earth. We notice it as we flip down the visor on our car to keep the glare out of our eyes. We notice it when we put on some sunscreen so we won't get a sunburn. We might gripe a bit when daylight savings time ends and it gets dark in the early evening.

Did you know that the mass of the sun is 330,000 times that of our earth? In fact, the sun is so large that about 1,300,000 earths could fit into it. What's more, the sun can warm our earth—providing the light and heat that is needed for us to survive—even though it is almost *93 million miles* away.

It is easy to miss the greatness of the sun and forget how huge it is. It is easy to overlook all of the benefits it brings. It is right there, every day . . . yet we hardly notice it.

The gospel of Jesus is the spiritual equivalent of the sun. It is bigger than we realize. The good news of Jesus and the message of the gospel is offered to *every human being* who has lived and ever will live. It has power to save *all* who will receive the grace extended by Jesus. It alone has the power to bring peace to the world and hope to those who are broken.

Although the gospel is deeply personal, it is not just about us, Jesus, and our Bible. This would be like comparing the sun to a candle. The gospel changes individual lives, but it also transforms families, communities, nations, and the world. It saves the lost and makes radically diverse people friends and family members. The gospel is *massive* in scope. This is why the best investment of our lives is to become servants of the gospel. It is bigger than we dream!

SHARE

Why is it dangerous to reduce the gospel to *only* the simple idea that it saves us from our sins and gives us a relationship with Jesus?

WATCH

Play the video segment for session four (see the streaming video access provided on the inside front cover). As you watch, use the following outline to record any thoughts or concepts that stand out to you.

We are never freer than when we surrender fully as servants of Jesus (Ephesians 3:1–8)

It is not about *do's* and *don'ts* but about what Jesus has done (Ephesians 3:9)

Our unity and togetherness tell the dark power of hell, you lost (Ephesians 3:10–11)

The gospel is much bigger than simply saying, "God forgave me of my personal sins," even though this is an important part of the gospel (Ephesians 3:12–13)

Adversity can be God's university of learning to walk closer with Jesus (Ephesians 3:12–13)

Prayer deepens our gratitude and grows our love (Ephesians 3:14–19)

True faith is about more than just us, Jesus, and our Bible (Ephesians 3:20)

Jesus gives us dynamite power through his resurrection and the presence of his Spirit (Ephesians 3:20–21)

DISCUSS

Take a few minutes with your group members to discuss what you just watched and explore these concepts in Scripture. Use the following questions to help guide your discussion.

1. What impacted you the most as you watched Derwin's teaching?

2. **Read Ephesians 3:1–6.** We are all servants of something. What are some of the common things in our world that lure us in and make us their servant? Why is being a servant of Jesus and his gospel better than any of these options?

3. **Read Ephesians 3:7–10.** When we walk in Christian community (in our lives, our family, and as his Church), how does this send a message to forces of hell that they have lost and Jesus has won? What messages do we send the world when we walk in unity, love, and become family with people from different and diverse backgrounds?

4. **Read Ephesians 3:11–13.** The adversity of this life can become God's university for us to learn and grow in deep and true faith. When was a time you faced trials, struggles, or suffering and God used it to grow your faith and draw you closer to Jesus?

5. **Read Ephesians 3:14–19.** When we are established in Christ and receive his love, our love for others deepens, and our actions follow. What are signs that we are increasing in love for God? For his diverse family? For the world Jesus loves and died to save?

6. **Read Ephesians 3:20–21.** God's resurrection power resides in his people and is like spiritual dynamite! How can your group members cheer you on and pray for you as you seek to unleash God's power in one of these areas of your life:

- Loving someone who is challenging to love?
- Forgiving someone who has wronged you?
- Showing compassion on someone who is hurting?
- Growing family ties with someone who is different than you?

MEMORIZE

Your memory verse this week is from Ephesians 3:7:

I became a servant of this gospel by the gift of God's grace given me through the working of his power.

Have everyone recite this verse out loud. Then ask for any volunteers who would like to say the verse from memory.

RESPOND

What will you take away from this session? What is one next step you can take as you seek to surrender your life to believe the gospel, share the gospel, and live in the power of the gospel?

PRAY

Close your group time by praying in any of the following directions:

- Praise God that his gospel has power to wash away your sins, restore you to fellowship with him, and open the door to heaven. Then lift up thanks that the gospel *also* heals families, breaks down barriers, transforms communities, and unleashes resurrection power in every area of life.

- Ask the Holy Spirit to empower you to make your time, resources, and dreams come in line with the gospel. Offer your whole life to the service of the gospel.
- Pray for the members of your small group to be rooted and established in God's love so fully that they have heavenly power to comprehend the massive nature of the love of Jesus.

SESSION FOUR

Reflect on the material you have covered in this session by engaging in the following between-session learning resources. Each week, you will begin by reviewing the key verse(s) to memorize for the session. During the next five days, you will have an opportunity to read a portion of Ephesians, reflect on what you learn, respond by taking action, journal some of your insights, and pray about what God has taught you. Finally, on the last day, you will review the key verse(s) and reflect on what you have learned for the week.

DAY 22

Memorize: Begin this week's personal study by reciting Ephesians 3:7:

> *I became a servant of this gospel by the gift of God's grace given me through the working of his power.*

Now try to say the verse from memory.

Reflect: Being a servant of God and sharing the gospel is an honor. It is not a burdensome weight to carry but a privilege given to his sons and daughters. We should pause every day and thank God for his grace that makes us worthy to bear his name and share his gospel. How have you been a servant of the gospel recently to the people in your world?

DAY 23

Read: Ephesians 3:1–6.

Reflect: If you enjoy books, stories, or movies that have twists, turns, and intrigue, then you know the excitement that comes when the pieces fall in place and the mystery is solved. After century upon century, the mystery of the gospel is solved right here in this passage. Through the grace of God revealed in Jesus—through his sacrifice on the cross and resurrection—the two divided groups of people were joined together. Gentiles and Jews became family, friends, one body, a loving community. These people from every tribe, race, and tongue were reconciled to each other to build a diverse family of faith. When you think of the gospel, do you see the salvation of individual people as the end of the gospel's work or the beginning?

Journal:

- How did God bring the truth of the gospel to you and help you embrace this life-changing message of salvation?
- Once you received and embraced the gospel, how did this new vision of life transform your dreams, your words, and your actions?

Pray: Pray for specific areas of your life where you are at odds with people who are different from you. Ask God to release the power of the gospel to humble your heart and give you courage to seek healthy, loving, harmonious relationships with these people.

DAY 24

Read: Ephesians 3:7–9.

Reflect: The apostle Paul never lost his amazement that God would use him to bear the message of the hope found in Jesus. Paul had been a Jesus-hater and church-destroyer before he met the risen Savior on the road to Damascus. He had led the execution of Christians and orchestrated the destruction of churches. This is why, on occasion, Paul would write things such as, "I am less than the least of all the Lord's people." It was not that Paul hated himself or failed to recognize the grace of God. He just knew his past and stood amazed that God would use him. What in the past has made you feel unworthy of receiving or sharing the good news of Jesus?

Journal:

- Why is Paul such a good example of God's grace and desire to use all sorts of people, from every background, as messengers of his gospel?
- How can Paul's example help you move past any roadblocks to sharing your faith and engaging more fully in being a servant of the gospel?

Pray: Thank God today that he uses all kinds of people to share his good news. Pray for courage to share the gospel—even though none of us is worthy of such a high calling.

DAY 25

Read: Ephesians 3:10–13.

Reflect: Ponder this spiritual reality: God's plan to reveal his wisdom to the spiritual authorities in the heavenly realms is *you*! Not you alone, of course, but you and every other follower of Jesus in the world. The Church, God's beautifully diverse and loving family, are his revelation of the gospel. When God's people are servants of the gospel—when we are transformed by his truth and when we walk in harmony—all the forces of hell get the message. Jesus won! They lost! God is on the throne and his people are filled with the Spirit. What do the forces of hell see when they look at the local church you attend?

Journal:
- Every local church can be a spiritual signpost that Jesus has won the victory. What are ways that you can help your church reveal the victory of Jesus and his gospel?
- Paul was suffering for the sake of the gospel. What are some of the ways that you have counted the cost of following Jesus and being a servant of his gospel?

Pray: Pray for your church to be so committed to the gospel and so transformed by it that the forces of hell will see a real-world picture of the victory of Jesus.

DAY 26

Read: Ephesians 3:14–19.

Reflect: How long, deep, wide, and high is God's love for you and every person he has created? What price did he pay to reveal his love? What did God give to save you from sin and death and invite you into his diverse family? God made you and crafted you in your mother's womb. He has his eyes on you every moment of every day. He knows everything about you—and still loves you. He sent his Son from heaven to find you and save you. God did this not only for you but also for every person who has ever lived. He is ready to lavish his grace on anyone who will receive his love, take his hand, and follow him as their Lord. What will help you remember the depth of God's love and live each day aware of how valuable you are to him?

Journal:
- What does it mean to be rooted and established in love? How can you live with a greater commitment to keep your life built on the foundation of God's love?

- What does it look like to be filled to the measure of the fullness of God? How can you open your life to a greater filling of his presence and power?

Pray: Pray the words of Ephesians 3:14–19 two or three times and seek to make this your prayer.

DAY 27

Read: Ephesians 3:20–21.

Reflect: To God be all glory! Not to ourselves, or our pastor, or the church we attend. Not to anyone or anything except God. As human beings, we like praise and glory. This is rooted in the nature of sin and is a temptation for all of us. But we need to fight back and refuse to be glory seekers. Instead, every day can be an adventure of giving God the glory and lifting praise to him. What are some of the situations in life where you tend to seek glory and praise for yourself?

Journal:

- How can you give glory and praise to God in the flow of a normal day?
- What can you do to resist the temptation to turn the focus and praise of people on yourself?

Pray: Lift up a prayer giving God praise and glory for everything that comes to mind. Take time and declare praise to God for his many blessings, for his creation, for his character, for his grace, and for so much more.

DAY 28

Memorize: Conclude this week's personal study by again reciting Ephesians 3:7:

I became a servant of this gospel by the gift of God's grace given me through the working of his power.

Now try to say the verse completely from memory.

Reflect: Without the power of Jesus, we could not be servants of his gospel. If it were not for God's power, we would not be saved! How has God provided strength in your life to live for him and serve him? What is one way that you can serve others this week?

LIFE IN GOD'S FAMILY

EPHESIANS 4:1–5:5

God's new race of grace is a family of holiness in Christ. What God commands is always supported by God's powerful provision.

WELCOME

Families have traditions, rules, and accepted behaviors. Some families gather for meals together at a set time around a table, where phones are not welcome and distractions are minimalized. Others eat on the run or while watching shows on a variety of devices. In some families, coming together for special events like Christmas, Easter, birthdays, and other occasions is so much a part of the family culture that no one would think of missing them.

There are families who understand there is an unstated rule to take off their shoes before going into the house. There are some where it is understood there is no playing ball in the house and that everyone needs to keep out of certain rooms reserved for special guests and special occasions. Other families have rules about the amount of time that is spent watching television, playing video games, and other "screen time." Every family has practices and behaviors that are part of their culture, and these vary from home to home.

God's family also has guidelines, rules, and commands that shape the behavior of its household members. If there was a poster on the refrigerator in the kitchen of God's house, it would have family rules like these listed:

- Be gentle and humble
- Love each other with patience
- Use your God-given abilities
- Grow up in spiritual maturity
- Be generous
- Speak truthfully
- Deal with anger and conflict
- Don't take what belongs to others
- Watch your words
- Show compassion
- Forgive like Jesus forgave you

God does not have a refrigerator, but if he did, Ephesians 4 could be posted as rules of the house. We would all be much better off if we followed these commands in our families, our community, in the workplace—and certainly in the family of God, his church.

SHARE

Tell about one tradition, practice, or rule that impacted how your family of origin functioned (for better or for worse).

WATCH

Play the video segment for session five (see the streaming video access provided on the inside front cover). As you watch, use the following outline to record any thoughts or concepts that stand out to you.

We are the family that God promised Abraham . . . and God loves his family

The dynamic structure of Ephesians:

Ephesians 1–3 is about *who we are as members of God's family*. There are more than twenty declarations about our identity.

Ephesians 4–6 is about *how God's people are to live.* There are more than thirty specific commands, rules, and guidelines.

We don't have to perform for God because Jesus is our "good enough"

God's new race of grace is characterized by holiness (Ephesians 4:1–6)

Every member of God's new race of grace is equipped for ministry (Ephesians 4:11–16)

God's family members are called to surrender their minds to Jesus (Ephesians 4:17–24)

God's people are called to imitate his good and holy example (Ephesians 4:25–5:5).

DISCUSS

Take a few minutes with your group members to discuss what you just watched and explore these concepts in Scripture. Use the following questions to help guide your discussion.

1. What impacted you the most as you watched Derwin's teaching?

2. The Holy Spirit inspired Paul to write about more than twenty different identities we have as members of God's family (see Ephesians 1–3) and then lay out more than thirty commands about how we are to live as God's people (see Ephesians 4–6). Why do you think God begins with who we are before he clarifies what he wants us to do?

3. **Read Ephesians 4:1–6.** Holiness is about being conformed to the pattern and person of Jesus Christ. What is one characteristic of Jesus that you want to be more and more

reflected in your life? What is one step you can take to part-ner with the Holy Spirit as he seeks to grow this attribute in your heart and life?

4. **Read Ephesians 4:9–13.** Derwin shared about God calling him to do something he would never have chosen. He grew up as a stutterer, but God called him to preach! Think about a call that God has placed on your life or something that he has led you to do that you would not have otherwise chosen. How has your faithfulness to follow God's leading brought him glory and been a blessing to others?

5. **Read Ephesians 4:17–24.** Paul draws a contrast between living in the Lord (following his will) and being dislocated from Jesus. What are some of the things in this world that can draw us away from living in God's will? How can we resist these enticements?

6. **Take a moment to review Ephesians 4:25–5:5.** In this pas-sage, God gives his family members a list of bad things to avoid doing and good things that we should be doing. What

is one commandment that jumps out at you that you know God wants you to follow with greater faithfulness? How can your group members pray for you and keep you accountable to grow in this area?

MEMORIZE

Your memory verse this week is from Ephesians 4:2:

Be completely humble and gentle; be patient, bearing with one another in love.

Have everyone recite this verse out loud. Then ask for any volunteers who would like to say the verse from memory.

RESPOND

What will you take away from this session? What is one practical next step you can take as you seek to be a contributing and valuable member of God's diverse and loving family?

PRAY

Close your group time by praying in any of the following directions:

- Thank God that he has clarified your identity and that your life of faith is an extension of who Jesus has made you to be (and who he is still making you to be).
- Pray that you will live with a deep and profound awareness that Jesus is your "good enough" and that your actions of faithfulness will be a response to God's grace and not an effort to get it (since you already have it in Jesus).
- Ask the Holy Spirit to empower each person in your small group to grow in holiness. Pray for them to take steps forward in the specific area of growth that they shared with the group.

SESSION FIVE

Reflect on the material you have covered in this session by engaging in the following between-session learning resources. Each week, you will begin by reviewing the key verse(s) to memorize for the session. During the next five days, you will have an opportunity to read a portion of Ephesians, reflect on what you learn, respond by taking action, journal some of your insights, and pray about what God has taught you. Finally, on the last day, you will review the key verse(s) and reflect on what you have learned for the week.

DAY 29

Memorize: Begin this week's personal study by reciting Ephesians 4:2:

Be completely humble and gentle; be patient, bearing with one another in love.

Now try to say the verse completely from memory.

Reflect: "Be completely humble and gentle." Not just a little humility. Not just occasional gentleness. In the power of Jesus, you can be *completely* humble and gentle. This is the call for members of God's family! Try to imagine what the Church could look like if every one of God's daughters and sons was growing in humility and gentleness. What is one area of your life where you need to grow a humble and gentle spirit? How have pride and a harsh spirit crept into your life? What can you do to battle against these attitudes and actions?

DAY 30

Read: Ephesians 4:1-6.

Reflect: There is one body—the body of Jesus Christ, his Church. In this body, dramatically diverse people are called to unity and a bond of peace. In our fragmented, conflicted, and polarized world, this can seem like a fantasy. How is this even possible? But it *is* absolutely possible and exactly what our Creator wants. God wants the world to see his Church so united, so living in harmony, and so filled with peace that they long for what God can bring. As followers of Jesus, we have the honor of living in this kind of community and inviting the world to join us. If a non-believer in your community were to attend your church for a couple of weeks, what signs of unity and peace would they witness in your congregation?

Journal:
- What are ways you can contribute to the unity and peace of your local church?
- How can you become a greater peacemaker?

Pray: Pray for your church (and other congregations in your community) to grow in unity and peace. Pray for pastors of different churches to model unity as they love each other, pray for each other, and partner for the sake of the gospel.

DAY 31

Read: Ephesians 4:7–12.

Reflect: What is the role of a church leader? What are pastors and teachers in the Church called to do for the glory of God?

One of the key responsibilities is to "equip God's people for works of service." In other words, the job of a church leader is not to do all the ministry. The call is to equip and support the church members as they discover, develop, and deploy their unique spiritual gifting. When this happens, a church has dozens, hundred, or thousands of ministers (servants) rather than just a few. If every Christian is a minister, and if every church leader equips them for acts of Jesus-honoring service, then we can change the world. This is exactly what God wants to do through us. So . . . are you being equipped and inspired to use your God-given gifts in some ministry that impacts your church, community, or the world?

Journal:
- What are ways that your church equips and inspires its members to discover, develop, and use their spiritual gifts?
- How does the body of Christ get built up as God's people exercise their spiritual gifts?

Pray: Pray for your church leaders to hear the call to equip all the members of your church for meaningful ministry. Also ask God to stir each person in your church to embrace their gifts and use them for the glory of Jesus.

DAY 32

Read: Ephesians 4:13–16.

Reflect: Every parent takes delight in watching their children grow up. When children excel in their physical, mental, or relational growth, the parents beam with pride and talk about their kids with their friends. But when the natural maturing process is stunted, the parents become concerned and seek out help. Our heavenly Father is concerned about the growth of his sons and daughters. This is why passages such as this one focus on the need for disciples of Christ to grow beyond spiritual infancy into full maturity. When we grow up, our heavenly Father celebrates! When you look at your life as a Christian and your relationship with God, do you see yourself in a growth season, stagnated, or slipping backward?

Journal:

- What is a next step you can take to grow in your faith? How will you take steps forward in this area of your journey with Jesus?
- What is one area you are growing in your relationship with Jesus? How will you celebrate this area and keep moving forward?

Pray: Confess areas of your life where you have been stalled in spiritual growth and pray for God to give you passion and power to change and get back on track.

DAY 33

Read: Ephesians 4:17–28.

Reflect: We can get stuck thinking in ways that resemble the world's thinking instead of having the mind of Christ. Paul calls this *futile* and *ignorant* thinking. This kind of mindset leads to a hard heart and a sinful lifestyle. But the good news is that as followers of Jesus and members of God's family, we don't have to live like the world. We don't have to be slaves to sin. Instead, we can take off the old ways and put on the new ways of our Savior. In the power of Jesus, we can turn away from falsehood, anger, dishonesty, and other behaviors that break the heart of God. We can learn to speak the truth, express anger in redemptive ways, and live in ways that glorify the Lord. What are some of the ways you have put off old bad habits and taken on a new and Jesus-honoring lifestyle? What transformation has the Holy Spirit brought into your life?

Journal:
- What does it mean to you to "put off your old self"?
- What does it mean to you to "put on the new self?" How has doing this made a difference in your life for how you relate to God and others?

Pray: Invite the Holy Spirit to search your heart and help you see any hidden attitudes, motives, or behaviors that need to be taken off and set aside. Ask for power to live in ways that bring glory to Jesus, health to his family, and joy in your life.

DAY 34

Read: Ephesians 4:29–5:5.

Reflect: Our words have power! Unwholesome talk, rage, and slander do more damage than we realize. In God's diverse family, there will always be challenges, differences, and opportunities to react with harshness instead of grace. This is why Paul advises us to watch our words when it comes to how we live in community. We need to be continually asking ourselves whether our words will *build up* the person we are addressing. If the answer is yes, we should speak. If the answer is no, we should pause, pray, or just stay silent. Who is a person you know who speaks grace-filled words consistently? What can you learn from his or her example?

Journal:
- When are you most tempted to let your words become harsh and hurtful?
- Who in your life needs you to speak words that build that person up? How can you bless that individual this week with your words?

Pray: Ask God to give you power to close your mouth when your words are going to be damaging and hurtful. Pray for wisdom as you seek to speak words that bring life, hope, and meet the needs of others.

DAY 35

Memorize: Conclude this week's personal study by again reciting Ephesians 4:2:

> *Be completely humble and gentle; be patient, bearing with one another in love.*

Now try to say the verse completely from memory.

Reflect: We are called to *bear* with each other. But there is a qualifier. We are to bear with each other *in love*. The concept of bearing with others presupposes that relationships—even in God's family—can be difficult. Loving people is hard, and the reality is there are just some people who are more challenging to love than others. God, in his grace, places people in our lives who will stretch us, who are different than us, and who will demand that we grow in grace. What next step can you take to bear a difficult person in your life and uplift him or her?

EMPOWERED TO STAND

EPHESIANS 5:6–6:24

God's multiethnic race of grace is characterized by his strength in us, not our own power. We are the family promised by Abraham. Our passionate love and unity sends shockwaves through the kingdom of darkness and reveals the victory of Jesus.

WELCOME

Forgetting can be fatal. Imagine that you were changing a flat tire on your car and you forgot to tighten the lug nuts all the way. You might not notice the error right away . . . but some day when you are heading down the freeway at 70 MPH, what was forgotten could prove to be costly. In the same way, it might not seem like a big deal when you remember to click your seatbelt, but the night you have a drowsy driver cut in front of you, it just might save your life!

In Paul's day, forgetting was just as fatal. No warrior would have dreamed of going into battle without first making sure they were fully prepared for battle. They tucked their tunic into their belt and pulled it nice and tight so they would not trip on it. They put on their breastplate to protect their vital organs. They made sure their sandals were laced up and they had a sure footing for any terrain. They had their shield in hand, ready to block arrows, stop sword thrusts, and deflect stones slung at high velocity. They fixed their helmet so their head and neck were protected. Every solider had their sword handy and sharp . . . prepared for defensive and offensive work. Forget even one of these, and the odds of victory go down substantially!

As Paul relates in this final section of Ephesians, in our battle against our spiritual enemy, forgetting to equip ourselves with the armor that *God* has provided can be just as deadly. He calls us as members of his family and fighting force to stand strong, resist the spiritual enemies who seek our destruction, and fight back in his power against the forces of hell. We have been empowered to stand and fortified with all we need for victory. The question is—are we ready? Do we remember, each day, to put on the armor, take up the sword, and prepare for victory?

SHARE

Tell about a time you forgot something important and explain the consequences you faced.

WATCH

Play the video segment for session six (see the streaming video access provided on the inside front cover). As you watch, use the following outline to record any thoughts or concepts that stand out to you.

As members of God's race of grace, we need to put on the armor of God (Ephesians 6:10–20)

We are called and equipped to stand against the devil and the dark powers

Don't leave your helmet in the locker room—or there will be pain ahead!

The devil wants division, but God is making diverse people into one beautiful family

Get ready for the battle, every day, by equipping with the . . .

Belt of truth—Jesus is the truth (Ephesians 6:14)

Breastplate of righteousness—Jesus is our righteousness (Ephesians 6:14)

Sandals of peace—Jesus gives us peace (Ephesians 6:15)

Shield of faith—our faith in Jesus (Ephesians 6:16)

Helmet of salvation—assurance of Jesus' saving power (Ephesians 6:17)

Sword of the Spirit—God's Word (Ephesians 6:17)

Pray that the gospel will go out and transform the world (Ephesians 6:18–19)

We have been blessed to be a blessing (Ephesians 6:20–24 and Genesis 12:1–3)

DISCUSS

Take a few minutes with your group members to discuss what you just watched and explore these concepts in Scripture. Use the following questions to help guide your discussion.

1. What impacted you the most as you watched Derwin's teaching?

2. **Read Ephesians 6:10–12.** What are some of the signs and indicators that make us aware there is a spiritual battle raging all around us? Why is it essential that we stay aware and tuned into the reality of this spiritual war?

3. **Read Ephesians 6:13–17.** Which of the pieces of your spiritual armor do you need to be more intentional to remember to put on each day:

   o Belt of truth—knowing with confidence that Jesus is the truth?
   o Breastplate of righteousness—living in the righteousness of Jesus?
   o Sandals of peace—walking in the peace of Jesus vertically and horizontally?
   o Shield of faith—keeping your faith in Jesus alive and strong?
   o Helmet of salvation—Living with absolute assurance of Jesus' saving power?

4. **Read Ephesians 6:17.** What step can you take in the coming weeks to increase your Bible reading, learning, and obedience to what God teaches you? How can your group members cheer you on and help you stay accountable to follow through on this?

5. **Read Ephesians 6:18–20.** As we have seen, Paul was in prison when he wrote this letter. Here, he asks the believers for prayer support. What did Paul ask the Ephesian church family to pray for him? Why do you think this was Paul's request?

6. **Read Ephesians 1:3 and Genesis 12:1–3.** God has blessed his family members with every spiritual blessing in the heavenly realms. In addition, he has blessed us so that we can be a blessing to the nations (all people from every imaginable background). What ways could we be a blessing to the world if we truly grew into a multiethnic, diverse, loving, united, beautiful family of believers? What is one next step you can take to seek unity with, and love for, all people (no matter their background)?

MEMORIZE

Your memory verse this week is from Ephesians 6:13:

> *Therefore put on the full armor of God, so that when the day of evil comes, you may be able to stand your ground, and after you have done everything, to stand.*

Have everyone recite this verse out loud. Then ask for any volunteers who would like to say the verse from memory.

RESPOND

What will you take away from this session? What is one practical next step you can take to stand strong and resist the enticements and lures of your spiritual enemy?

PRAY

Close your group time by praying in any of the following directions:

- Thank God for the beautiful diversity of his people. Pray that his unity will mark your life and our churches in such a way that the world looks on and longs for what only God can create.
- Pray for the Holy Spirit to nudge, whisper, and remind you to put on the full armor of God every day so that you can stand strong.
- Ask God to grow your love for his Word so much that you will have a longing to be a Bible-binger and not a Scripture-snacker.

SESSION SIX

Reflect on the material you have covered in this session by engaging in the following between-session learning resources. Each week, you will begin by reviewing the key verse(s) to memorize for the session. During the next three days, you will have an opportunity to read a portion of Ephesians, reflect on what you learn, respond by taking action, journal some of your insights, and pray about what God has taught you. Finally, on the last day, you will review the key verse(s) and reflect on what you have learned for the week.

DAY 36

Memorize: Begin this week's personal study by reciting Ephesians 6:13:

> *Therefore put on the full armor of God, so that when the day of evil comes, you may be able to stand your ground, and after you have done everything, to stand.*

Now try to say the verse completely from memory.

Reflect: Don't cut corners here. When it comes to the armor you need to fight the dark powers of hell, put on every single piece every single day. The apostle Paul is clear. He does not say "*if* the day of evil comes" but "*when* the day of evil comes." The battle is real, it is serious, and you will only live in victory if you are fully prepared and ready to stand. What can you do to remind yourself to put on the full armor of God as you begin each day?

DAY 37

Read: Ephesians 5:6–20.

Reflect: It is fair to say that we live in a world with a huge potential for distraction and wasted time. With powerful computers, phones, and tablets, we can find ourselves falling into an addictive rabbit hole of entertainment, distractions, and consumption. Our world has become an entertainment culture. Of course, there is nothing inherently wrong with some time for play, hobbies, or enjoying a good show. But our lives are short, and we have been given a mission from our God. Paul, inspired by the Holy Spirit, calls each of us to be conscious about how we use our time—to make the most of every opportunity and not be foolish with our days. How do these words resonate with you? How are you making the most of your days?

Journal:

- What are one or two things you do (these can be good things or bad things) that take up a lot of time but don't produce much in the way of spiritual growth? Write down a couple of these "time-wasters." Be honest about how much time you spend in a normal week or month doing these things that burn up your time but do very little to make an eternal impact on the world around you.
- What are a couple of shifts you can make in your life to decrease the wasted time and increase engagement in things that really matter?

Pray: Pray for power to cut back on things that are time consumers and yield little fruit for the glory of God or for blessing other people in your life.

DAY 38

Read: Ephesians 5:21–6:9.

Reflect: In this section of Ephesians, we find what scholars call a *household code*. God inspired Paul to give wisdom for how people should conduct themselves in a family and household setting. In the ancient world, a normal household would include a married man and woman, children and parents, and also household servants. God was serious about homes becoming a haven of grace! As we read Paul's words, it is important to recognize that neither God nor Paul were endorsing or affirming the institution of slavery or indentured servants. What Paul was acknowledging was that this practice was a huge part of the ancient world—and God wanted every person in a household to be treated with grace, kindness, and love. What stands out to you the most as you read these instructions for households?

Journal:
- What are practices and behaviors that you could engage in to better make your household a place of love, harmony, and glory to Jesus?

- What are some things you should start or stop in the coming week to strengthen the relationships among the people to whom you are closest?

Pray: Pray for yourself and the people you live with or are closest to. Ask God to help you live with grace, humility, and a commitment to be gracious to the people in your household.

DAY 39

Read: Ephesians 6:10–24.

Reflect: We all have daily habits. We brush our teeth every day (more than once). We eat every day (sometimes three or more meals). Most people take in some kind of media each day (more than once). Daily habits are normal and valuable, as long as the habits are good ones. In the same way, if we are going to fight the forces of darkness and walk in victory, we need to have one additional good spiritual habit. It might be one of the most valuable habits we can begin. *We need to put on the full armor of God and prepare for battle.* We can do this by reading this passage each morning and praying for each piece of armor to stay in place. In the process, we can think through our day and ask God to empower us to walk in his victory all day long. What is the best time for you to put on the armor of God on a daily basis? How will you do this?

Journal:
- What are some of the places you are facing temptation and spiritual attacks?
- Are there any ways you are leaving a door open to the enemy in this area of your life? What can you do to slam the door shut and keep it closed?

Pray: Pray for diligence and discipline as you seek to make preparing for daily spiritual battles a normal part of the rhythm of your day.

DAY 40

Memorize: Conclude your forty-day personal study by again reciting Ephesians 6:13:

> *Therefore put on the full armor of God, so that when the day of evil comes, you may be able to stand your ground, and after you have done everything, to stand.*

Now try to say this verse completely from memory.

Reflect: *Stand. Stand. Stand. Stand.* Did you notice this word appears four times in just four verses? In the ancient world, the way a writer emphasized a point was to repeat it, repeat it, and repeat it again. As you conclude this forty-day journey through the book of Ephesians, ask yourself these questions and allow the Holy Spirit to whisper his truth into your heart: *What can you do to stand as a uniter in God's diverse family? How can you stand fully clothed in the armor of God for the battles ahead? How can you stand against anything that seeks to divide God's people and destroy its unity? How will you stand in the joy of the Lord and celebrate the beautiful multiethnic race of grace that God is making into his forever family?*

LEADER'S GUIDE

Thank you for your willingness to lead your group through this study! What you have chosen to do is valuable and will make a great difference in the lives of others. The rewards of being a leader are different from those of participating, and we hope that as you lead you will find your own walk with Jesus deepened by this experience.

This study on Ephesians in the *40 Days Through the Book* series is built around video content and small-group interaction. As the group leader, think of yourself as the host. Your job is to take care of your guests by managing the behind-the-scenes details so that when everyone arrives, they can enjoy their time together. As the leader, your role is not to answer all the questions or reteach the content—the video and study guide will do that work. Your role is to guide the experience and cultivate your group into a teaching community. This will make it a place for members to process, question, and reflect on the teaching.

Before your first meeting, make sure everyone has a copy of the study guide. This will keep everyone on the same page and help the process run more smoothly. If members are unable to purchase the guide, arrange it so they can share with other members. Giving everyone access to the material will position this study to be as rewarding as possible. Everyone should feel free to write in his or her study guide and bring it to group every week.

SETTING UP THE GROUP

Your group will need to determine how long you want to meet each week so you can plan your time accordingly. Generally, most groups like to meet for either sixty minutes or ninety minutes, so you could use one of the following schedules:

SECTION	60 MINUTES	90 MINUTES
WELCOME (members arrive and get settled)	5 minutes	5 minutes
SHARE (discuss one of the opening questions for the session)	5 minutes	10 minutes
READ (discuss the questions based on the Scripture reading for the session)	5 minutes	10 minutes
WATCH (watch the video teaching material together and take notes)	15 minutes	15 minutes
DISCUSS (discuss the Bible study questions based on the video teaching)	25 minutes	40 minutes
RESPOND/PRAY (reflect on the key insights, pray together, and dismiss)	5 minutes	10 minutes

As the group leader, you will want to create an environment that encourages sharing and learning. A church sanctuary or formal classroom may not be as ideal as a living room, because those locations can feel formal and less intimate. No matter what setting you choose, provide enough comfortable seating for everyone, and, if possible, arrange the seats in a semicircle so everyone can see the video easily. This will make the transition between the video and group conversation more efficient and natural.

Also, try to get to the meeting site early so you can greet participants as they arrive. Simple refreshments create a welcoming atmosphere and can be a wonderful addition to a group study. Try to take food and pet allergies into account to make your guests as comfortable as possible. You may also want to consider offering childcare to couples with children who want to attend. Finally, be sure your media technology is working properly. Managing these details up front will make the rest of your group experience flow smoothly and provide a welcoming space in which to engage the content of this study on the book of Ephesians.

STARTING THE GROUP TIME

Once everyone has arrived, it is time to begin the study. Here are some simple tips to make your group time healthy, enjoyable, and effective.

Begin the meeting with a short prayer and remind the group members to put their phones on silent. This is a way to make sure you can all be present with one another and with God. Next, give each person a few minutes to respond to the questions in the "Share" section. This won't require as much time in session one, but beginning in session two, people may need more time to share their insights from their personal studies. Usually, you won't answer the discussion questions yourself, but you should go first with the "Share" questions, answering briefly and with a reasonable amount of transparency.

At the end of session one, invite the group members to complete the "Your 40-Day Journey" for that week. Explain that they can share any insights the following week before the video teaching. Let them know it's not a problem if they can't get to these activities some weeks. It will still be beneficial for them to hear from the other participants in the group.

LEADING THE DISCUSSION TIME

Now that the group is engaged, watch the video and respond with some directed small-group discussion. Encourage the group members to participate in the discussion, but make sure they know this is not mandatory for the group, so as to not make them feel pressured to come up with an answer. As the discussion progresses, follow up with comments such as, "Tell me more about that," or, "Why did you answer that way?" This will allow the group participants to deepen their reflections and invite a meaningful conversation in a nonthreatening way.

Note that you have been given multiple questions to use in each session, and you do not have to use them all or even follow them in order. Feel free to pick and choose questions based on the needs of your group or how the conversation is flowing. Also, don't be afraid of silence. Offering a question and allowing up to thirty seconds of silence is okay. This space allows people to think about how they want to respond and gives them time to do so.

As group leader, you are the boundary keeper for your group. Do not let anyone (yourself included) dominate the group time. Keep an eye out for group members who might be tempted to "attack" folks they disagree with or try to "fix" those having struggles. These kinds of behaviors can derail a group's momentum, so they need to be steered in a different direction. Model active listening and encourage everyone in your group to do the same. This will make your group time a safe space and create a positive community.

The group discussion leads to a closing time of individual reflection and prayer. Encourage the participants to review what they have learned and write down their thoughts to the "Respond" section. Close by taking a few minutes to pray as directed as a group.

Thank you again for taking the time to lead your group. You are making a difference in the lives of others and having an impact on the kingdom of God!

4▶ DAYS THROUGH THE BOOK

Study Books of the Bible
with Trusted Pastors

The 40 Days Through the Book series has been designed to help believers more actively engage with God's Word. Each study encourages participants to read through one book in the New Testament at least once during the course of 40 days and provides them with:

- A clear understanding of the background and culture in which the book was written,

- Insights into key passages of Scripture, and

- Clear applications and takeaways from the particular book that participants can apply to their lives.

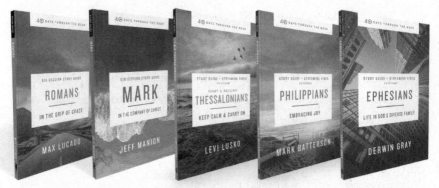

ROMANS	In the Grip of Grace	Max Lucado
MARK	In the Company of Christ	Jeff Manion
FIRST & SECOND THESSALONIANS	Keep Calm & Carry On	Levi Lusko
PHILIPPIANS	Embracing Joy	Mark Batterson
EPHESIANS	Life In God's Diverse Family	Derwin Gray

Available now at your favorite bookstore,
or streaming video on StudyGateway.com.

 Harper*Christian*
Resources